THE *love* revealed

CHALLENGE

*45 Days to Discovering God's Authentic Love*

KERRY CLARENSAU

 Influence

www.InfluenceResources.com

Published by Influence Resources
1445 N. Boonville Ave., Springfield, Missouri 65802

Published in association with The Quadrivium Group—Orlando, FL
info@TheQuadriviumGroup.com
and New Vantage Partners—Franklin, TN
info@NewVantagePartners.net

Cover design by Archetype Brands—Springfield, MO
Interior design and typesetting by Wellspring Design and Jay Victor—Nashville, TN

ISBN: 978-1-936699-10-0

First printing 2011

Printed in United States of America

# dedication

This book is dedicated to all the women who have revealed God's love to me.

# acknowledgements

Thank you to those who worked diligently to make the *Love Revealed* project a success. To the authors of *Love Revealed:* Jodi Detrick, Joanna Weaver, Janelle Hail, and JoAnn Butrin—I count it a privilege to work alongside you.

To the Influence Resources staff, your continued encouragement and commitment to this project has exceeded my expectations. Thank you for making the process of writing a joy!

And to Angela Moody, for designing the artwork I had in my heart!

# introduction

Welcome to the *Love Revealed Challenge*, companion to the *Love Revealed* Bible study.

The thoughts offered in this challenge are designed to help you apply the principles of *Love Revealed* in a practical way. Each day offers a Scripture Point, a Thought Point, and a Challenge Point.

You may choose to use this challenge:

- ♥ As an individual, 45-day devotional,
- ♥ With a friend, using the Thought Points as discussion guides, or
- ♥ In a small group setting, meeting weekly to discuss the material.

We pray the Holy Spirit will reveal God's love for you in transforming ways throughout this 45-day challenge. And that His love will brim over from your heart to everyone around you!

I

# day 1
## unfailing love

**Scripture Point**

"Your unfailing love, O LORD, is as vast as the heavens; your faithfulness reaches beyond the clouds. Your righteousness is like the mighty mountains, your justice like the ocean depths. You care for people and animals alike, O LORD. How precious is your unfailing love, O God! All humanity finds shelter in the shadow of your wings" (Psalm 36:5–7, NLT).

**Thought Point**

David, the writer of this psalm, enjoyed a close relationship with God and was called a man after God's own heart. He wrote many psalms describing the greatest of God's love for us. Take time to reread this psalm and thoughtfully consider how God's love is described in every line.

♥ What does it mean to you that God's love is unfailing?

## Challenge Point

Spend a few minutes in one of your favorite places in nature today. Consider how God's love is displayed all around you. Then take some time to express your love for Him in your own unique way:

♥ Write your own psalm describing God's unfailing love;
♥ Paint or draw something in nature that speaks of God's faithfulness;
♥ Sing a song that shares your gratefulness for His goodness;
♥ Simply speak aloud your praise.

Allow His unfailing love to wash over your every thought and care.

_____

_____

_____

_____

## day 2
## sacrificial love

**Scripture Point**

"This is how we've come to understand and experience love: Christ sacrificed his life for us. This is why we ought to live sacrificially for our fellow believers, and not just be out for ourselves" (I John 3:16, THE MESSAGE).

**Thought Point**

Many times we love others conditionally—only loving those who love us back. But Christ's love for us didn't depend upon our responses or on our worthiness. Although He knew some would accept Him and others would reject Him, still He loved us and gave His life for us. It is difficult to accurately explain that kind of love. In chapter one, Kerry describes God's love as being greater than the love of a mother for her child. Most mothers willingly sacrifice whatever is necessary for their children. We are called to love one another in the same sacrificial way.

♥ Think about the sacrificial nature of a new mother's love for her infant and compare it to God's love for us.

♥ What hinders us from loving others this way?

## Challenge Point

Look for a way to encourage someone by sacrificing some of your time and energy today—loving them in a Christ-like way. Here are some ideas to get your creative energies flowing:

♥ Babysit for a single mom or give a couple a night out;

♥ Clean the home of someone who is in a busy season of life;

♥ Help a neighbor with some yard work;

♥ Make a meal for a friend or offer to do her grocery shopping;

♥ Spend some time with someone who is homebound.

# day 3
# lavishing love

**Scripture Point**

"See what great love the Father has lavished on us, that we should be called children of God! And that is what we are!" (I John 3:1, NIV).

**Thought Point**

While there are no perfect earthly parents, moms and dads reveal their love for their children by providing shelter and care to the best of their ability. As followers of Christ, we are the children of God, with a Heavenly Father who is completely flawless. He is all-powerful, all-knowing, always with us, faithful, worthy of our trust, full of mercy, and able to love us perfectly. First John 3:1 tells us this perfect God *lavishes* His love on His children. His love is evident all around us—through the faithfulness of every sunrise and the seasons, in the balance of nature, in our daily provisions, through the love of others, through His Word, and in our circumstances.

♥ Take some time to meditate on the character of God.
♥ Considering the character of our Heavenly Father, what are the benefits of being His child?

## Challenge Point

Memorize I John 3:I and think about it often throughout your day. God is love and He is continually revealing His love to His children—through nature, other people, our circumstances, and His Word. Ask Him to help you recognize His love today in a special way. In the space below write out some of the ways He reveals His love.

_____

_____

_____

_____

_____

_____

## day 4
# love in action

**Scripture Point**

"But if anyone has this world's goods (resources for sustaining life) and sees his brother and fellow believer in need, yet closes his heart of compassion against him, how can the love of God live and remain in him? Little children, let us not love [merely] in theory or in speech but in deed and in truth (in practice and in sincerity)" (I John 3:17, 18, AMP).

**Thought Point**

God can work and meet the needs of people any way He chooses. But many times He wants to use us, His followers, to meet the needs of those around us. This verse helps us to understand that love is an *action*, not simply words or a good feeling.

God blesses our lives so we can bless others. If we think our possessions are simply the product of our own initiative, we can become stingy. But when we remember everything we have is a gift from God, it is easier to share with others. We are simply sharing His goodness!

♥ Think about a time when God met your needs through the kindness of a friend or family member. How did you feel?

♥ What do you have that you can share?

## Challenge Point

Consider how you can use your resources to help people who are struggling financially. Here are some ideas to get your creative energies flowing:

♥ Make them a meal;

♥ Buy them groceries, toiletries, or basic cleaning supplies;

♥ Buy them a gas gift card;

♥ Give them some of your clothing or extra household items;

♥ Take them shopping for something they need.

## day 5
# continuous love

**Scripture Point**

"Dear friends, let us continue to love one another, for love comes from God. Anyone who loves is a child of God and knows God. But anyone who does not love does not know God, for God is love. God showed how much he loved us by sending his one and only Son into the world so that we might have eternal life through him. This is real love—not that we loved God, but that he loved us and sent his Son as a sacrifice to take away our sins" (1 John 4:7–10, NLT).

**Thought Point**

If we lose the wonder of God's love for us and take for granted the gift of forgiveness, we can become apathetic about showing God's love to others. This verse tells us clearly that when we don't love others, we are revealing we don't really know and love God. We should do a regular self-test and ask ourselves honestly—*am I consistently loving others? Would the people in my life say, "She really loves me"?*

We can live continually in the fullness of His love by acknowledging His goodness and forgiveness in our lives. With that type of humility, we are able to allow His love to pour through our lives to those around us.

- ♥ What are some ways you can live continually accepting His love and forgiveness?
- ♥ How can you make loving others a priority in your life?

## Challenge Point

Make a list of the people you come into contact with most days—your family, coworkers, and friends. Take a few minutes to honestly ask yourself about each one of them, "Would _____ say that I love them?" Make a fresh commitment to live in His love and allow it to pour through you to each person in your life.

## day 6
# encouraging love

**Scripture Point**
"So encourage each other and build each other up"
(1 Thessalonians 5:11, NLT).

**Thought Point**
Everyone loves to be around encouragers! They
energize us and motivate us to keep growing and
serving. This verse challenges us to intentionally
find ways to build others up. Our love for others is
revealed when we truly want what is best for them,
and we do what we can to help them experience
God's goodness.

Encouragement can be expressed in many ways—
by our life of faith, our words, assistance we offer,
and even our presence.

♥　Think about a time when someone's
encouragement made a specific impact in

your life. How would you describe the difference it made?

♥ List the different ways you are encouraged by others.

## Challenge Point

Cheer someone on today! Ask the Lord to lead you to someone who needs encouragement and believe He will show you what you can do for her. Throughout the day watch your words and tone of voice, making sure everything you say builds others up. At the end of the day, rate yourself on a scale from 1 to 10—1 being discouraging and 10 being very encouraging.

_____

_____

_____

_____

_____

_____

_____

_____

# day 7
## love others

**Scripture Point**

"We love because he first loved us. Whoever claims to love God yet hates a brother or sister is a liar. For whoever does not love their brother and sister, whom they have seen, cannot love God, whom they have not seen. And he has given us this command: Anyone who loves God must also love their brother and sister" (I John 4:19–21, NIV).

**Thought Point**

Many people claim to love God, yet they have visible animosity for people in their life. This Scripture is clear—we can't love God and hate others.

In Matthew 25:34–40, Jesus explains how our love for others is a direct reflection of our love or lack of love for God. He tells us that when we feed the hungry, give a drink to someone who is thirsty, take in a stranger, or visit the prisoner, we are doing it for Him. Our love for Him is evident in our love and care for others.

♥ Consider the idea that when we are loving and serving others, we are loving and serving Christ. How does this idea impact your treatment of others?

♥ How can you keep this truth in focus as you interact with others?

## Challenge Point

Read Matthew 25:31–46. Then take some time today to honestly ask yourself what your treatment of others is saying about your relationship with God. If there is any hate in your heart, confess it, and ask the Lord to help you love the way He loves us.

_____

_____

_____

_____

_____

_____

## day 8
### love invites

**Scripture Point**
"Always be eager to practice hospitality" (Romans 12:13b, NLT).

**Thought Point**
Some people have an incredible gift of hospitality. They are able to create an inviting atmosphere, a delicious meal, and engaging conversation with ease. But we don't have to be Martha Stewart to make someone feel special in our homes. A simple act like inviting a friend to join us for a long conversation and a hot cup of coffee can be an effective way to reveal our love for her.

When we invite people into our homes, we are displaying our desire to serve them by sharing what we have.

♥ Describe the feeling of walking into someone's home when they have prepared a special meal and taken care of every detail for your visit.

♥ Why do you think God's Word encourages us to practice hospitality?

## Challenge Point

This week invite someone into your home for dessert or a simple meal. From the moment you invite them, help them to feel welcomed and honored in your home. Plan the details with them in mind. Consider their schedule, their likes, and their interests. When you are together, focus more on them than on yourself. If you are unable to have them into your home, invite them for a picnic in the park, or for coffee at a neighborhood café. But even if you are not in your home, treat them as an honored guest.

_____

_____

_____

_____

## day 9
# there is no fear in love

**Scripture Point**

"God is love. When we take up permanent residence in a life of love, we live in God and God lives in us. This way, love has the run of the house, becomes at home and mature in us, so that we're free of worry on Judgment Day—our standing in the world is identical with Christ's. There is no room in love for fear. Well-formed love banishes fear. Since fear is crippling, a fearful life—fear of death, fear of judgment—is one not yet fully formed in love" (I John 4:18, THE MESSAGE).

**Thought Point**

Fear is an important emotion, helping us to know when to move away from dangerous situations. But there is a big difference in healthy fear and allowing fear to grip our hearts. Our response to fear is important—we can run into the arms of our Heavenly Father and allow His love to drive away our anxiety. Think about a small child crossing a busy street, hand-in-hand with his big, strong, loving father. In his simple trust, he isn't afraid of the endangering traffic. He believes his dad won't let him get hurt. As we come to really know the full character of God and His unfailing love for us, we can walk through this life and even face death with the kind of trust the small child has with his daddy.

♥ How can understanding the character of God and His unfailing love for you help you to live free from fear?

## Challenge Point

Read the New International Version of I John 4:18. Then write, "Perfect love drives out fear" someplace where you will see it throughout your day (consider making it the background of your computer). Honestly ask yourself if you are allowing anxiety to consume your heart. Admit each concern to your loving, Heavenly Father. Ask Him to reveal His love in a way to help you live without fear.

## day 10
# reveal love to your leaders

**Scripture Point**

"Dear brothers and sisters, honor those who are your leaders in the Lord's work. They work hard among you and give you spiritual guidance. Show them great respect and wholehearted love because of their work" (1 Thessalonians 5:12,13, NLT).

**Thought Point**

Several times in the Scriptures we are admonished to honor our leaders. Our "changed lives" are the best gifts we can give to them, but we should take time to intentionally show them our love and appreciation. When we follow this instruction and honor those who lead us, we are also loving God with our obedience.

♥ Who are the people who have made an impact in your spiritual life? Your pastor? Small group leader? Parent? Friend? Mentor? Do they know how much you appreciate them?

♥ How do you feel when someone expresses appreciation to you?

♥ How does respect demonstrate love?

## Challenge Point

Don't wait for a special occasion. Take time today to reveal your love for at least one person who has given you spiritual guidance. Here are a few ideas:

♥ Send her an e-mail or card expressing appreciation for something specific she has taught you;

♥ Buy her a meaningful gift;

♥ If this is a particularly busy season for her, do something to meet a practical need—take her a meal, babysit for her children, help her around the house;

♥ Ask how you can help her this week.

## day 11
# live in His love

**Scripture Point**

"But you, dear friends, carefully build yourselves up in this most holy faith by praying in the Holy Spirit, staying right at the center of God's love, keeping your arms open and outstretched, ready for the mercy of our Master, Jesus Christ. This is the unending life, the real life!" (Jude 20,21, THE MESSAGE).

**Thought Point**

God loves us completely and unconditionally, but we have the responsibility to receive and live in His love. Chapter 6 of *Love Revealed* encourages us to "practice the presence of God"—to live with an awareness of God's presence. Even though we know He is always with us, we have a tendency to neglect the relationship He offers. The same is true of His love. We can have the head-knowledge

of His affection for us, but we may not keep our
heart "right at the center of God's love."

♥ Consider what it means for you to "keep
your arms open and outstretched, ready
for the mercy of Jesus."

## Challenge Point

Today be mindful of all of the ways God reveals
His love for you. He might:

♥ Remind you of His love through a
Scripture;
♥ Show you kindness through a friend or
family member;
♥ Provide for your daily needs;
♥ Reveal His faithfulness through a sunrise
or something else in nature;
♥ Make His presence known through inner
peace.

Before the day is over write a thank-you note to
God for the ways He reveals His love to you today.

## day 12
# love celebrates

**Scripture Point**

"Be happy with those who are happy" (Romans 12:15a, NLT).

**Thought Point**

Life includes moments of joy and moments of sorrow. Ecclesiastes 3:4 tells us there is "a time to weep and a time to laugh, a time to mourn and a time to dance." It is important to embrace every day for what it has to offer. We should take time to celebrate the good things in life. Our celebrations can even be a way of praising God for the gifts He brings into our lives. Without recognizing and enjoying the happy moments, life can get out of balance with work and responsibilities.

♥ What can happen if we never take time to celebrate the good things in life?

## Challenge Point

Are you taking time to celebrate the happy moments in life? Make a fresh commitment to celebrate with those you love in the coming months. Start today by sending a card to someone who has something to celebrate—a graduation, retirement, new baby, marriage, anniversary, a new job, a work-related victory, a new house, etc. If it is someone in your immediate family or circle of friends, consider throwing a simple party—take the time to celebrate together!

_____

_____

_____

_____

_____

_____

_____

_____

_____

_____

_____

_____

## day 13
# His loving care

**Scripture Point**

"Give all your worries and cares to God, for he cares about you" (I Peter 5:7, NLT).

**Thought Point**

God cares about everything that touches your life, and He knows things about you no one else knows, like the number of hairs on your head. He hasn't promised a life free from concerns, but He has promised to never leave us alone to carry our "stuff" by ourselves. He wants to help us with each and every situation we face. He wants to give us His strength for the trials we walk through. He wants to comfort us in our sorrow. He wants to give us wisdom for the difficult situations in our families. He wants to give us insight for the challenges in our work. He really cares about every detail of our lives!

♥  How has God revealed His care for you
   in the past?
♥  How can those experiences encourage you
   to give Him your worries about today?

## Challenge Point

On a 3x5 card write out your current worries and
cares, and literally place them before the Lord in
prayer. Allow His peace to flood your heart and
mind today in a fresh, new way as you meditate
on His great care for you. On the reverse side of
the card, write out today's Scripture to remind you
of His love.

_____

_____

_____

_____

_____

_____

_____

_____

_____

## day 14
# love weeps

**Scripture Point**

"Weep with those who weep" (Romans 12:15b, NLT).

**Thought Point**

Life is marked with seasons of "weeping" caused by loss. When we think of loss, we may immediately think of the death of a loved one. Death is one of the greatest sorrows in this life. But loss is also experienced in other ways—the loss of a job, a relationship, a home, a marriage, or a dream. Transitional times of life, like the empty nest, can also feel like loss. And as we age, we experience seasons of letting go along the way, like the loss of physical strength and independence. All of these are times of "weeping." We reveal our love for our family and friends when we weep with them.

♥ How can we lighten the load of a grieving friend by weeping with her?

## Challenge Point

If you have a friend or a loved one who is mourning a loss, ask the Lord for a creative way to "weep with them" today. Maybe you can help to ease her pain and lighten the load of sorrow by:

♥ Sending a card or thoughtful e-mail.
♥ Taking her a meal or groceries.
♥ Taking care of a household responsibility.
♥ Performing a simple act of kindness.
♥ Spending time with her.

_____

_____

_____

_____

_____

_____

_____

_____

## day 15
# communicate love

**Scripture Point**

"May the words of my mouth and the meditation of my heart be pleasing to you, O LORD, my rock and my redeemer" (Psalm 19:14, NLT).

**Thought Point**

Consider all of the ways we communicate—the words we speak are only a portion of what we "say." Our attitudes, body language, tone, volume, and expressions actually say more than our words. The thoughts and feelings we allow to settle in our hearts are conveyed in every word we speak and the way we say those words. If we are irritated or judgmental, it is noticeable in a prideful attitude, rigid body language, and harsh tone. But the opposite is also true—if our thoughts and heart are full of God's love, His grace is evident in the words we say and the way we communicate them.

♥ Think about how you communicate when you are self-focused and impatient.

♥ How can God's love be revealed through your body language, tone, volume, and expressions?

## Challenge Point

Let the prayer of this simple verse be your prayer today. Intentionally check your body language, facial expression, tone of voice, and also the words you speak. Make sure everything you are expressing reveals God's love. Ask a close friend to give you honest feedback. At the end of the day, honestly assess if your words and thoughts were pleasing to God.

_____

_____

_____

_____

_____

_____

_____

# day 16
## love's obligation

**Scripture Point**

"Owe nothing to anyone—except for your obligation to love one another. If you love your neighbor, you will fulfill the requirements of God's law" (Romans 13:8, NLT).

**Thought Point**

Did you notice this verse says loving others is actually an *obligation?* It is not a suggestion. Love is the practical way we live obediently to God. Think about the ways loving others fulfills the requirements of God's law. If you love your neighbors, you won't steal from them, lie about them, or hurt them in any way. Instead you will want what is best for them, and you will do whatever you can to help them experience it.

## Challenge Point

Spend a few minutes today thanking God for the people who love you. Take some time to acknowledge their love for you and return their love in a special way. You might want to:

- ♥ Surprise them by an act of service;
- ♥ Change your schedule to spend extra time with them;
- ♥ Write them a thank-you note for their love;
- ♥ Take them to their favorite restaurant or coffee shop;
- ♥ Buy them something you know they would enjoy.

_____

_____

_____

_____

_____

_____

_____

# day 17
## love doesn't complain

### Scripture Point

"Do everything without complaining and arguing, so that no one can criticize you. Live clean, innocent lives as children of God, shining like bright lights in a world full of crooked and perverse people" (Philippians 2:14,15, NLT).

### Thought Point

It is common for some of us to *grumble* our way through life. When we are asked how we are doing, we might be tempted to list all of our woes. Even if we try not to complain, we can find ourselves describing how busy we are, as if we deserve a medal of honor for all we do. While it may be the norm in our society, it is important for us to remember that complaints and arguments are signs of self-centeredness and ungratefulness. Did you notice how the passage above describes those who don't complain? It says they shine like bright lights among perverse people. We can reveal our love for God by getting rid of our complaining, argumentative spirits.

♥ How can you fall into the complaining trap? When do you find yourself being the most argumentative?

♥ How do women who do everything without complaining shine like bright lights?

## Challenge Point

Make a small poster with the phrase, "Do everything without grumbling or arguing." Every time you grumble, complain, or argue, place a sticky note on the poster. At the end of the day review how you did. Make a fresh commitment to reveal your gratefulness and love for God by doing everything without complaining.

_____

_____

_____

# day 18
## love overcomes differences

**Scripture Point**

"Don't be selfish; don't try to impress others. Be humble, thinking of others as better than yourselves" (Philippians 2:3, NLT).

**Thought Point**

In Chapter 2 of *Love Revealed*, Jodi talked about "differentness" and how it hinders our ability to connect with others. If we surround ourselves with people who are very similar to us, we actually stifle our growth and become self-centered. Everyone benefits from having many different types of relationships. While we can enjoy spending time with our peers, it is important to learn by being with people who are more experienced than we are. We also gain different perspectives by hanging out with people who are older or younger. We become more compassionate when we have relationships with people who have special needs. And we can make a difference in someone's life when we connect with someone who has less experience than we do.

♥ How does humility enable us to form relationships with those who are different from us?

♥ Why are we uncomfortable around those who are different from us?

## Challenge Point

Take an inventory of your relationships. Are most of them your age? Do you all have similar interests and experiences? After reading the Thought Points above, do you realize you might need to establish other relationships? Has God placed someone in your daily life that is very different from you? Have you resisted connecting with her? Do something today to get to know that person better. Take time to pray specifically for her and commit to connecting with her in an intentional way in the coming weeks.

## day 19
# love's golden rule

**Scripture Point**

Jesus said, "Do to others whatever you would like them to do to you. This is the essence of all that is taught in the law and the prophets" (Matthew 7:12, NLT).

**Thought Point**

What a challenging command—to always treat others the way we want to be treated. Most often our first response to a negative encounter with someone is a reaction of our flesh. When someone is unkind to us, we want to return the "favor." We may justify our response by thinking, *They are getting what they deserve; if they were nice to me, I'd be nice to them.*

However, Jesus challenges us to treat others the way we would want to be treated, regardless of how they treat us. Have you ever considered that our treatment of others says more about our character than the behavior of the other person? When we make statements like, "She made me so mad, I couldn't help myself...," we are simply revealing our lack of self-control. We must own our responses and not hand the keys of our attitudes and reactions over to other people.

♥ When are you most likely to allow someone's behavior to negatively affect your responses?

♥ What adjustments can you make to better control your behavior?

## Challenge Point

Repeat this verse throughout the day, and allow its meaning to sink into your heart. In every encounter, think more about the other person than you think about yourself. Ask yourself, *if I were she, how would I want to be treated in this moment?* And then make sure your response fully represents the other's best interest. At the close of the day, review the responses of people when you treated them the way you would want to be treated—with kindness, dignity, concern, and respect.

# love's response

## Scripture Point

"Don't hit back; discover beauty in everyone. If you've got it in you, get along with everybody. Don't insist on getting even; that's not for you to do. 'I'll do the judging,' says God. 'I'll take care of it.' Our Scriptures tell us that if you see your enemy hungry, go buy that person lunch, or if he's thirsty, get him a drink. Your generosity will surprise him with goodness. Don't let evil get the best of you; get the best of evil by doing good" (Romans 12:19–21, THE MESSAGE).

## Thought Point

Everyone has been offended. Our natural tendency toward those who offend us is to get revenge. But vengeance ties us to the offense and weighs us down. Trying to get even creates feelings of bitterness. These negative feelings don't right the wrong or change the offender, but they can destroy us. Retaliation always creates a negative cycle in relationships—you hurt me, I hurt you, you hurt me.... We may think that simply ignoring our enemies is good enough. However, this Scripture encourages us to go beyond ignoring them and tells us to bless them. By blessing them we are freed from the offense.

- ♥ How does blessing our enemies reveal the love of Christ?
- ♥ How does blessing our enemies free us from destructive patterns?

## Challenge Point

The list below suggests some ways to bless those who have offended you.

- ♥ Don't tell others about the offense. Talking about it exposes their faults and discredits their character. Remember, we are to love our enemies (1 Peter 4:8).
- ♥ Pray for them (Matthew 5:44).
- ♥ Be at peace with them (Romans 12:18).
- ♥ Forgive them (Matthew 6:14,15).

# day 21
## love listens

**Scripture Point**

"Understand this, my dear brothers and sisters: You must all be quick to listen, slow to speak, and slow to get angry" (James 1:19, NLT).

**Thought Point**

Most of the time our natural inclination is to be slow to listen, quick to speak, and quick to get angry. But I Corinthians 13:4–7 tells us that, "Love is patient, love is kind. It does not envy, it does not boast, it is not proud. It does not dishonor others, it is not self-seeking, it is not easily angered, it keeps no record of wrongs. Love does not delight in evil but rejoices with the truth. It always protects, always trusts, always hopes, always perseveres." When we truly love others it will be evident in patience and kindness—we will be quick to listen, slow to speak, and slow to get angry.

♥ Think about the ways your conversations with others reveal what is in your heart.

♥ How is love demonstrated for someone when you are quick to listen? Slow to speak? Slow to get angry?

## Challenge Point

Choose to allow the Holy Spirit to speak through you today. When you find that your flesh is beginning to respond, bite your tongue. Be silent until the Holy Spirit speaks words of love through you. Remember that love is not proud or easily angered. At the end of the day, write out below what your responses revealed about your love for others.

_____

_____

_____

_____

_____

_____

_____

_____

# gracious love

**Scripture Point**

"Live wisely among those who are not believers, and make the most of every opportunity. Let your conversation be gracious and attractive so that you will have the right response for everyone" (Colossians 4:5,6, NLT).

**Thought Point**

As our relationship with Christ grows, our character becomes more like His. It is important for people to see His presence in our responses. These verses tell us our conversations with those who don't follow Christ should be gracious and attractive. As they witness His love, kindness, peace, joy, purpose, and contentment, they will be attracted to Christ *in* us.

♥ Have you ever met someone and knew they were "religious," but like the Pharisees, they were harsh and judgmental?

♥ Have you ever met someone, and within a few minutes you knew they were true followers of Christ? What characteristics revealed this truth?

## Challenge Point

Write "Let your conversation be gracious and attractive" on a piece of paper. If you have a camera phone, take a picture of the verse and make it the background on your phone. In every encounter today, make sure your responses are accurately representing Christ's goodness and love. Ask the Lord to show you someone to whom you can reveal His love in an ongoing way. Make a commitment to make the "most of every opportunity" He provides for you to interact with that individual.

_____

_____

_____

_____

## day 23
# rejoicing love

**Scripture Point**

"For the LORD your God is living among you. He is a mighty savior. He will take delight in you with gladness. With his love, he will calm all your fears. He will rejoice over you with joyful songs" (Zephaniah 3:17, NLT).

**Thought Point**

Think about the giggles and claps of parents and grandparents when their baby crawls to them for the first time. It is a time for rejoicing and absolute delight! Zephaniah 3:17 is written for those who run to God and trust Him (also read Zephaniah 3:12). He loves us so intensely that He actually celebrates those moments when we seek Him with all of our hearts. For a few moments, just consider what it means for God to take delight in you and rejoice over you with songs.

♥ How does it make you feel to know God delights in you and rejoices over you with joyful songs?

♥ How can His love calm all your fears?

## Challenge Point

Reread Zephaniah 3:17, and write the portion of the verse that is most meaningful for you somewhere you will see it throughout the day. Strive to seek and trust Him today with child-like faith in every situation. Consider how He might be rejoicing over you today. Share this verse with those you love.

_____

_____

_____

_____

_____

_____

_____

_____

_____

# day 24
## love honors

**Scripture Point**

"Love must be sincere. Hate what is evil; cling to what is good. Love each other with genuine affection, and take delight in honoring each other" (Romans 12:9,10, NIV).

**Thought Point**

We live in a day when flattery and disrespect are demonstrated all around us: *An employee flatters her boss, hoping for a raise. A student is demeaning to a peer, trying to feel better about herself.* But when our love is sincere, we think less about ourselves, and we truly want what is best for others. Genuine affection and honor flow from that type of sincere love.

♥  How have you seen genuine affection in action?
♥  What are some ways we can demonstrate honor?

## Challenge Point

Ask the Lord for a creative idea to demonstrate genuine affection for one person in your family. Then make the time today to shower him or her with your love, keeping in mind the way he or she best receives love. Prayerfully consider how you can "take *delight*" in honoring every member of your immediate family in the coming weeks—write out an action plan to help you follow through.

_____

_____

_____

_____

_____

_____

_____

_____

_____

_____

_____

_____

_____

# day 25
## love's first commandment

**Scripture Point**

"And you must love the LORD your God with all your heart, all your soul, all your mind, and all your strength" (Mark 12:30, NLT).

**Thought Point**

The first time we see the command to love God with all of our heart, soul, mind, and strength is in Deuteronomy 6:5. God's plan has always been for us to enjoy a close connection with Him. When Jesus was asked what the greatest command was, He responded with these same words, to love God! We were created for a vibrant relationship with God—to really know Him, to walk with Him every moment, and to love Him in a way that consumes us.

♥ How would you describe loving God with all of your heart? With all your soul? With all of your mind? With all of your strength?

## Challenge Point

Because we are all unique, our individual relationships with God will look different from others. Write "Loving God is my greatest responsibility," and put it on your mirror or refrigerator door. Consider what it means for you personally to love God as described in Mark 12:30. Write a letter to God revealing your commitment to love Him more every day.

_____

_____

_____

_____

_____

_____

_____

_____

# love helps

## Scripture Point

"When God's people are in need, be ready to help them" (Romans 12:13a, NLT).

## Thought Point

Everyone experiences times of need—things break down, our bodies get sick, we can lose our jobs, accidents happen, and relationships can struggle. We also live in a time when natural disasters are occurring all around us. When trouble strikes, people's lives can be completely changed in an instant. During these moments of need, we should be ready to help. We can allow God's goodness to flow through our lives in a way that clearly demonstrates His love.

♥ Describe a time when you saw God's love revealed through people meeting the needs of those around them.

## Challenge Point

Prayerfully consider how you can meet a practical need of someone you love. Take at least one action step toward meeting that need today. You may want to consider supporting or volunteering for an organization that offers disaster relief, such as Convoy of Hope. Or contact your church to see how you can give on a regular basis to assist those who are struggling to meet their daily needs.

_____

_____

_____

_____

_____

_____

_____

_____

_____

_____

_____

_____

_____

## day 27
# love seeks

**Scripture Point**

"Those who know your name trust in you, for you, LORD, have never forsaken those who seek you" (Psalm 9:10, NIV).

**Thought Point**

The word "seek" means to look for, search for, or try to find. God obviously wants us to know Him, because He makes wonderful promises to those who seek Him. One of the best ways to find God is to prioritize time alone with Him every day—reading His Word and talking with Him. When we take the time to focus specifically on Him, we are able to continue in His presence throughout the busyness of our day.

♥ How has spending time alone in God's presence helped you to trust Him more?

## Challenge Point

Read the following verses and write out the promises God makes to those who seek Him:

♥ Deuteronomy 4:29,
♥ I Chronicles 28:9,
♥ 2 Chronicles 7:14,
♥ Psalm 34:10,
♥ Jeremiah 29:13,
♥ Matthew 7:7,8,
♥ Hebrews 11:6.

Make a fresh commitment to spending time alone with Him every day.

_____

_____

_____

_____

_____

_____

_____

_____

# love serves

## Scripture Point

"After washing their feet, he put on his robe again and sat down and asked, 'Do you understand what I was doing? You call me "Teacher" and "Lord," and you are right, because that's what I am. And since I, your Lord and Teacher, have washed your feet, you ought to wash each other's feet. I have given you an example to follow. Do as I have done to you'" (John 13:12–15, NLT).

## Thought Point

The story of Jesus washing the feet of His closest friends starts in John 13:1, "Jesus knew that the hour had come for him to leave this world and go to the Father. Having loved his own who were in the world, he loved them to the end." After washing their feet, He encourages them to love one another the same way. Then He promises God will bless them when they do.

Think about what it was like for Jesus, the Son of God, to wash 12 men's feet. Keep in mind they walked everywhere on dirt roads—24 dusty feet and 240 grimy toes! Can you imagine a more humbling act of service?

♥ What do you think Jesus was teaching His disciples about love?

♥ What do you think He wants you to understand through this story?

## Challenge Point

Read John 13:1–17. Consider the extent of His love as He took off His outer clothing, wrapped a towel around His waist, got on the floor, and took their feet into His hands. Look for a humble task to complete today—maybe something no one else wants to do. And do it with great love for the One who washed the feet of His closest friends.

_____

_____

_____

_____

## day 29
# obedient love

**Scripture Point**

"But those who obey God's word truly show how completely they love him. That is how we know we are living in him" (I John 2:5, NLT).

**Thought Point**

Our love for God is seen most clearly in our behavior—obedience flows naturally from those who love Him deeply. *But how can we deepen our love for God?* One of the best ways is to spend more time with Him. He is always with us, but we are not aware of Him. We can go all day without giving Him much thought, so we must strive to live every moment acknowledging His presence. Then we can continue in constant communion with Him throughout our day. Brother Lawrence called it a "secret conversation of the soul." We can thank Him for His goodness, ask Him for help, or simply enjoy His company. This type of close relationship with God will guide our thoughts, words, and actions, helping us to live in a way that pleases Him.

♥ How can you be more aware of God's presence today?

♥ How will being aware of God's presence help you to obey Him?

## Challenge Point

Strive to be aware of Him in every thought, attitude, word, and action. Write "Love Obeys" on a sticky note and place it on your computer screen to see it throughout the day. Let it remind you that obedience reveals your love for God. At the end of the day, consider how being intentionally aware of God's presence impacted your decisions and responses.

_____

_____

_____

_____

_____

# day 30
# love doesn't condemn

## Scripture Point

"So let's stop condemning each other. Decide instead to live in such a way that you will not cause another believer to stumble and fall" (Romans 14:13, NLT).

## Thought Point

Romans 14 starts off by encouraging us to, "Accept him whose faith is weak, without passing judgment on disputable matters." Verse 13 challenges us to be more focused on living our own lives, than on condemning others.

We waste time and energy by judging those around us, because we are incapable of changing their behavior. The only actions we can control are our own. *The Message* translates the passage this way:

"Forget about deciding what's right for each other. Here's what you need to be concerned about: that you don't get in the way of someone else, making life more difficult than it already is." That is mature love, being concerned with how our responses will impact others.

♥ Why are we tempted to pass judgment on others' behaviors?

## Challenge Point

Every time you are tempted to think critical thoughts of someone today, turn the spotlight on yourself. Make sure there is nothing in your life to cause someone else to stumble. Make a fresh commitment to live free from critical thinking and judgmental attitudes. Be determined to reveal God's love in everything you do.

_____

_____

_____

_____

_____

# day 31
## love works

**Scripture Point**

"Work willingly at whatever you do, as though you were working for the Lord rather than for people" (Colossians 3:23, NLT).

**Thought Point**

Have you looked closely at this passage? It says that *whatever* we are doing we can do for the Lord! This means we can do laundry, mow the grass, write an article, and balance the checkbook for Him! As we remember that we are working for *Him*, we will be more diligent and strive for excellence in everything we do.

Consider what it would be like for Jesus to physically be in your home and workplace. What would it be like to fix a meal for Him or make His bed?

♥ How would you complete each work assignment differently if He were standing next to you today?

♥ Would His presence impact your attitudes, behaviors, and words?

## Challenge Point

Use one of your talents to express your love for God today. Whether you are a baker, artist, writer, housekeeper, teacher, physician, or musician, do something purely out of your love for God. Write "All for Him" in your online calendar, and set reminders to prompt you throughout the day. Strive to do everything as if He were standing next to you.

_____

_____

_____

_____

_____

_____

_____

## day 32
# dress in love

**Scripture Point**

"So, chosen by God for this new life of love, dress in the wardrobe God picked out for you: compassion, kindness, humility, quiet strength, discipline. Be even-tempered, content with second place, quick to forgive an offense. Forgive as quickly and completely as the Master forgave you. And regardless of what else you put on, wear love. It's your basic, all-purpose garment. Never be without it" (Colossians 3:12–14, THE MESSAGE).

**Thought Point**

Every day is marked by some kind of trouble— our alarm doesn't go off, our kids make a mess, or someone cuts us off in traffic. While trouble is inevitable, our response is always up to us. We can allow our flesh to be the first responder, or we can allow God's love to flow through us. This passage challenges us to *choose* compassion, kindness, humility, quiet strength, and discipline. Each of these are responses wrapped in the right attitude. We can choose to show compassion over indifference, kindness over rudeness, quiet strength over harshness, and discipline over annoyance.

♥   What are some practical ways you can "wear love" when trouble comes your way?

## Challenge Point

As you dress today, speak the words of Colossians: "Today I choose to wear compassion, kindness, humility, quiet strength, and discipline." Think of your spiritual wardrobe throughout the day. Remember that you are chosen by God for this new life of love—allow His love to flow through every response. At the end of the day, ask yourself if your behavior revealed God's love.

_____

_____

_____

_____

_____

# day 33
## think love

**Scripture Point**

"Summing it all up, friends, I'd say you'll do best by filling your minds and meditating on things true, noble, reputable, authentic, compelling, gracious—the best, not the worst; the beautiful, not the ugly; things to praise, not things to curse" (Philippians 4:8, THE MESSAGE).

**Thought Point**

Our thoughts are important! What we allow to fill our thoughts will work its way to our attitudes and eventually our behaviors. But the freeing reality is, we get to choose what we think about.

When we decide to meditate on God's truth and love, we will be able to live in a way that is pleasing to Him. In Philippians 4:8, the Apostle Paul gives us a great list of things we can choose to fill our thoughts—things that are true, honest, pure, and lovely. We can intentionally meditate on the blessings God has given us, and intentionally turn away from thoughts of discontentment.

♥ Describe how the things we think about impact our attitudes and behaviors, both positively and negatively.

## Challenge Point

Live today, aware of your thoughts. Remember, you can choose what you allow yourself to think about. When you have negative thoughts, find a Scripture to align your thoughts with His Word. Take time to journal how the verses corrected your thinking.

_____

_____

_____

_____

_____

_____

_____

# day 34
## love defends

**Scripture Point**

"Pure and genuine religion in the sight of God the Father means caring for orphans and widows in their distress and refusing to let the world corrupt you" (James 1:27, NLT).

**Thought Point**

Most of us will walk through times when we are alone or vulnerable. Scripture challenges us to take care of one another in those times of weakness. Psalm 82:3 tells us to, "Defend the weak and the fatherless; uphold the cause of the poor and the oppressed." This is one of the clearest ways God's love is revealed in the world—when His children care for those who are at risk or underserved.

♥  Describe the evidence of God's love in the care of the defenseless.

## Challenge Point

Read Isaiah 58:6–11 and consider the challenge and promises of this passage. Then identify someone you know who is currently in a vulnerable time of life. It could be an elderly aunt living alone or a child whose parents are making poor life choices. Ask the Lord how you could care for her or him in the coming weeks and take one action step today.

_____

_____

_____

_____

_____

_____

_____

_____

_____

_____

_____

_____

_____

# day 35
## love's provision

**Scripture Point**

"The LORD is my shepherd; I have all that I need. He lets me rest in green meadows; he leads me beside peaceful streams. He renews my strength. He guides me along right paths, bringing honor to his name. Even when I walk through the darkest valley, I will not be afraid, for you are close beside me. Your rod and your staff protect and comfort me" (Psalm 23:1–4, NLT).

**Thought Point**

This passage describes some of the ways God reveals His love for us: He meets our needs, provides rest, leads, restores, renews, guides, stays close, protects, and comforts. What a beautiful revelation of His great love! Reread Psalm 23 (if you have access to other translations, read it in several versions) and carefully consider each line.

♥ Think about all of the ways God cares for you.

## Challenge Point

Identify one need in your life. Maybe you need direction, provision, or comfort. Use biblegateway.com or a concordance to look up verses about the ways God desires to meet your specific need. Write out the verse that speaks most clearly to your situation. Keep your mind on the truth of this verse throughout the day, and allow His peace to fill your heart (Isaiah 26:3).

_____

_____

_____

_____

_____

_____

_____

_____

_____

# day 36
## love covers

**Scripture Point**

"Above all, love each other deeply, because love covers over a multitude of sins" (I Peter 4:8, NIV).

**Thought Point**

Love covers; it doesn't expose! In moments of frustration, we may be tempted to talk to others about the faults or mistakes of the people we love. And sometimes we even use others' weaknesses for our entertainment—telling how our brother can't even change a light bulb or our sister doesn't know when to stop talking. But one of the greatest gifts we can give to those we love deeply is the assurance we will never speak negatively about them to others. When they can trust that their weaknesses, mistakes, and faults won't be broadcasted from our lips, they will feel loved—because love covers!

♥ We have all felt exposed by the careless words of someone we are close to. Think about how you feel when it happens to you.

♥ Hopefully, we have all been "covered" by someone's love. Think about how you feel in those moments.

## Challenge Point

Identify someone who has loved you by "covering your sin." Write her a thank-you note expressing your gratitude. Then identify someone who might need this kind of love from you and consider what it will look like to love her deeply.

_____

_____

_____

_____

_____

_____

_____

_____

# day 37
## love rejoices

**Scripture Point**

"Rejoice in the Lord always, I will say it again: Rejoice!" (Philippians 4:4, NIV).

**Thought Point**

We may ask ourselves, *Can God really command an emotion? Do we have control over the amount of joy we experience?* Isaiah 55 provides insight on the idea of experiencing joy. Verses 1–3 promise us that through hearing God's Word we can experience His love and find satisfaction for our thirsty souls. The chapter also challenges us to seek the Lord, find forgiveness for our sins, and to trust God's ways even when we don't understand what is happening in our lives. Then Isaiah reveals this promise for those who seek the Lord, "You will go out in joy and be led forth in peace" (Isaiah 55:12, NIV).

♥  Think about how experiencing forgiveness and God's faithful love will bring
   satisfaction and joy.

♥  How can your decision to "rejoice" reveal
   your love for God?

## Challenge Point

Read Isaiah 55 and consider how the thirsty,
joy-starved soul is renewed. Then identify the
relationships or circumstances where you struggle
the most to rejoice. Ask God to help you discover
His love in each of those situations.

_____

_____

_____

_____

_____

_____

_____

_____

_____

_____

## day 38
# love isn't "me first"

**Scripture Point**

"Love never gives up. Love cares more for others than for self. Love doesn't want what it doesn't have. Love doesn't strut, Doesn't have a swelled head, Doesn't force itself on others, Isn't always 'me first,' Doesn't fly off the handle, Doesn't keep score of the sins of others, Doesn't revel when others grovel, Takes pleasure in the flowering of truth, Puts up with anything, Trusts God always, Always looks for the best, Never looks back, But keeps going to the end" (I Corinthians 13:4–7, THE MESSAGE).

**Thought Point**

When we use our own standards or the ideas of our society, we may think we are a loving person. But this passage clearly defines the way God wants us to love—not focused on ourselves, but honestly wanting the best for others. Love is much more than a warm, fuzzy feeling. It is a desire to see God's best in someone's life and being willing to do what is necessary for him or her to experience that goodness. Read I Corinthians 13 in your favorite translation of the Bible. Take some time to carefully consider every statement about love.

♥    How does this description of love mirror God's love for us?

## Challenge Point

Read I Corinthians 13:4–7 and replace your name for the word *love* (i.e., "Ashley never gives up, Ashley cares more for others than for herself,...) As you read those statements aloud, give yourself a quick assessment, and admit where you have difficulty loving. Then ask God to help you love in a way that more closely resembles I Corinthians 13.

_____

_____

_____

_____

_____

day 39
# love prays

**Scripture Point**

"Don't fret or worry. Instead of worrying, pray. Let petitions and praises shape your worries into prayers, letting God know your concerns. Before you know it, a sense of God's wholeness, everything coming together for good, will come and settle you down. It's wonderful what happens when Christ displaces worry at the center of your life" (Philippians 4:6,7, THE MESSAGE).

**Thought Point**

Worry is simply mentally rehearsing the possible negative outcomes to the difficulties we face. *Everyone* has something they could worry about. But spending our time and emotional energy worrying doesn't accomplish anything. It only produces anxiety, which can make us physically sick—another reason for worry. What a vicious cycle! Thankfully this verse doesn't simply tell us not to worry, it gives us valuable instructions for living in God's love and experiencing His peace.

♥ Worry is the natural response to trouble. According to Philippians 4:6,7, how can we turn that natural response into a life-giving prayer?

## Challenge Point

Allow the first hint of worry to remind you to pray. Take some time today to pray about every need in your life. Then list ten ways God has revealed His love to you and blessed your life in the past. Thank Him for each blessing. As you remember what He has already done, allow those memories to build your faith. Ask for His peace to flood your heart and protect your mind from anxiety.

_____

_____

_____

_____

_____

_____

# day 40
## simple love

**Scripture Point**
"Do everything in love" (I Corinthians 16:14, NIV).

**Thought Point**
It really doesn't get more simple than this—*do everything in love.* While these four words seem so basic, they summarize every directive we receive in the New Testament. Living by this verse will completely change our lives, so let's think about it one word at a time. "Do" implies that our lives will have tasks to complete. "Everything" encompasses every task from the mundane to the monumental. And "in love" reveals the desired motive for every task, no matter how big or small.

Remember, it is the small decisions that reveal our faithfulness and enable God to trust us with more. When our love for God and others motivates everything we do, even the simple tasks become worship, and the mundane things in life have renewed meaning.

♥ How can we view our daily tasks differently when they are done in love?

## Challenge Point

Identify three seemingly mundane, daily tasks—like doing the dishes, driving the kids to school, making dinner, etc. Focus on your love for God and the people you serve as you complete them today. At the end of the day describe how each task was different as you did them "in love."

_____

_____

_____

_____

_____

_____

_____

_____

# love doesn't doubt

**Scripture Point**

"No power in the sky above or in the earth below—indeed, nothing in all creation will ever be able to separate us from the love of God that is revealed in Christ Jesus our Lord" (Romans 8:39, NLT).

**Thought Point**

When we walk through difficult circumstances, we may wonder where God is and even question His love for us. Sometimes we allow our hurt, disappointment, and confusion to keep us from spending time with Him. But when we do that, we keep ourselves from relying on His ever-present love. Instead of running from God, we can run to Him with every doubt and concern. While He may not answer every question, if we rely on Him, He will reveal His unfailing love for us when we need it the most.

- ♥ How has doubt impacted your relationship with God?
- ♥ When have you questioned His love for you?

## Challenge Point

If you are in a time of realizing God's love for you, identify your favorite song or psalm about God's love. Then sing it or recite it to Him throughout the day. If you are in a season of questioning His love, honestly ask yourself if you have been running *from* Him or *to* Him? Take some time today to make the first step toward His ever-present love. Tell Him exactly how you are feeling. (Don't worry, He can take it! And He already knows.) Ask Him to help you see His love in the midst of your doubts.

_____

_____

_____

_____

_____

## day 42
# love speaks

**Scripture Point**

"Don't use foul or abusive language. Let everything you say be good and helpful, so that your words will be an encouragement to those who hear them. And do not bring sorrow to God's Holy Spirit by the way you live. Remember, he has identified you as his own, guaranteeing that you will be saved on the day of redemption. Get rid of all bitterness, rage, anger, harsh words, and slander, as well as all types of evil behavior. Instead, be kind to each other, tenderhearted, forgiving one another, just as God through Christ has forgiven you" (Ephesians 4:29-32, NLT).

**Thought Point**

Words carry a lot of weight. Most of us have heard the saying, "Sticks and stones may break my bones, but words will never hurt me." But this simply isn't true. Words can hurt! Some of our deepest wounds aren't from physical injuries but from careless words that have been hurled at us.

Understanding the impact of hurtful words, someone said, "If you can't say something kind, don't say anything at all." Kind, compassionate words have the ability to encourage others and build them up.

♥ How do kind and compassionate words reveal our love for others?
♥ Think about a time when someone's words were healing for you.

## Challenge Point

Today be aware of the words you speak. Make sure they will benefit those who hear them. If you are in the midst of a conflict with someone, use your words today to take the first steps toward healing the relationship.

_____

_____

_____

## day 43
# love's depth

**Scripture Point**

"I pray that from his glorious, unlimited resources he will empower you with inner strength through his Spirit. Then Christ will make his home in your hearts as you trust in him. Your roots will grow down into God's love and keep you strong. And may you have the power to understand, as all God's people should, how wide, how long, how high, and how deep his love is. May you experience the love of Christ, though it is too great to understand fully. Then you will be made complete with all the fullness of life and power that comes from God" (Ephesians 3:16-19, NLT).

**Thought Point**

In this passage, Paul is praying for the believers in Ephesus to really live in God's love. Listen to how *The Message* translates the last half of this passage: "And I ask him that with both feet planted firmly on love, you'll be able to take in with all followers of Jesus the extravagant dimensions of Christ's love. Reach out and experience the breadth! Test its length! Plumb the depths! Rise to the heights! Live full lives, full in the fullness of God."

♥ How do those verses make you want to respond to God's love?

♥ Try to describe the full lives that are available to those who experience this type of love.

## Challenge Point

Take some time to consider the greatness of God's love. Journal below by describing the various ways God has revealed His love to you. Share your thoughts with a close friend.

_____

_____

_____

_____

_____

## day 44
# love's place

**Scripture Point**

"He makes the whole body fit together perfectly. As each part does its own special work, it helps the other parts grow, so that the whole body is healthy and growing and full of love" (Ephesians 4:16, NLT).

**Thought Point**

Romans 12 tells us every believer is given specific gifts to serve others within the church. A few of these gifts are serving, teaching, encouraging, giving, leading, and showing mercy. All of the gifts are equally important. Ephesians 4:16 helps us to understand that each person's contribution is important for the overall health and growth of the church. May the challenge in I Corinthians 15:58 (THE MESSAGE) encourage us: "With all this going for us, my dear, dear friends, stand your ground. And don't hold back. Throw yourselves into the work of the Master, confident that nothing you do for him is a waste of time or effort."

♥ What gifts do you have that can bless your local church?

## Challenge Point

Talk to a leader in your church about where you might use your gifts to serve. If you are already serving, make a fresh commitment to allow God's love to be more clearly seen in your efforts of ministry.

_____

_____

_____

_____

_____

_____

_____

_____

_____

_____

_____

# day 45
## love revealed

**Scripture Point**

"And this is my prayer: that your love may abound more and more in knowledge and depth of insight, so that you may be able to discern what is best and may be pure and blameless for the day of Christ, filled with the fruit of righteousness that comes through Jesus Christ—to the glory and praise of God" (Philippians 1:9–11, NIV).

**Thought Points**

As our love for God deepens, our love and hunger for His Word grows. And our love for God grows as we discipline ourselves to read the Bible. It is a life-giving cycle!

It is important for us to understand that He desires to speak into our lives—and the main way He does that is through the Bible. He comforts us, gives us insights, changes our perspectives, and directs our decisions as we spend time reading His written Word. He literally transforms our lives with His Word.

♥ How does committing yourself to read the Bible reveal your love for God?

## Challenge Point

Read Psalm 119:9–16, and answer this question: What does this psalm teach you about God's Word? Find time today to read all of Psalm 119 to discover the benefits of reading and meditating on God's Word. Make a fresh commitment to read the Bible every day, and adjust your schedule to create the time it requires. Even if it feels like discipline at first, stick with it. You won't be sorry!

_____

_____

_____

_____

_____

_____

_____